Scout Jokes

Jokes

A collection of clean jokes and stories related to Scouting, camping and hiking

Thomas Mercaldo

Printed in the United States.
Seventh Printing
National Edition

Aquinas Scout Books
C/O Thomas C. Mercaldo
154 Herbert Street
Milford, CT 06461

BoyScoutBooks@aol.com

Scout Fun Books is not officially affiliated with the Boy Scouts of America, Girl Scouts of America, Scouts Canada or the World Organization of Scouting.

Scout Fun Books can be purchased on a wholesale basis for resale in Camp Stores, Scout Shops and Trading Posts. For details write to us at the above address or contact us by email at BoyScoutBooks@aol.com.

Preface

I have learned during my years in Scouting, that not all jokes are created equally. Scout Jokes is a collection of some of the funniest good clean jokes that have been shared along wilderness trails. It is the fifth in a series of books aimed at adding to the fun of the Scouting experience. Scout Jokes features many of the characters that you may have come to know in earlier books like Joe Scout, Jester, Chief Sequassen, Trader Jack, The Ranger, Joe Beagle Scout, The Scoutmaster and the Wild Adirondack Cow. Even if you are unfamiliar with Sequassen Secrets, Scout Riddles, Scout Skits, Scoutmaster's Minutes and Superior Campfires, you are sure to enjoy the humor presented in Scout Jokes.

Thank you for helping to make the Scout Fun Book series a success. I sincerely hope your entire troop enjoys the fun and adventure of Scout Jokes.

Tom Mercaldo

Table of Contents

Scout Stories

An American Scout troop was visiting Russia. Their guide's name was Rudolph, a staunch red communist, and throughout the trip, the Scoutmaster and Rudolph argued about everything starting with their differing political views. As the troop was getting ready to leave, the Scoutmaster said, "Look, it's starting to snow."

The guide immediately disagreed, "No, sir, it's raining out."

"I still think it's snowing," said the Scoutmaster.

The Scoutmaster's wife, weary of all this bickering interrupted the battle.

"I think Rudolph the Red knows rain dear."

***

A scoutmaster decided to use some psychology to try to get his lazy scouts to do some work. So he said, "I've got a nice easy job for the laziest Scout here. Any volunteers?"

In an instant all but one of the Scouts raised their hands. "Why didn't you raise your hand," the Scoutmaster asked him?

"Too much work," he replied.

A deer and an antelope were wandering through camp late one night. Suddenly, the antelope stopped and cocked his head. "What's the matter," asked the deer.

The antelope answered, "I thought I just heard a discouraging word."

***

When Troop 10 visited the zoo, the zookeeper was very upset because the gnu's had separated into two groups. One group was always fighting while the other group always got along. He wanted to get rid of the group that fought because there's no gnu's like good gnu's.

A Scout Leader was sick and tired of constantly answering ridiculous questions from his Tenderfoot Scouts. So finally, he instituted a rule, that anyone who asked a question that he himself couldn't answer, would have to wash everyone else's mess kit after supper.

This didn't stop Jester Scout who asked more questions than anyone else. He asked, "When a chipmunk digs its hole, how come it doesn't leave a pile of dirt around the entrance?"

"Answer it yourself," the troop chimed gleefully.

"A chipmunk starts digging its hole from the inside," Jester explained.

The Scoutmaster looked at him incredulously, and asked, "How could he get to the inside to start digging?"

"You made the rule," Jester answered, "you answer or start washing."

***

A group of Scouts sat down for dinner at summer camp. One of the new boys was about to ask someone to pass him the bread, when one of the Scouts stood up and yelled "63" and everyone in the room laughed. Another Scout called out "29" and the whole room went into hysterics. The new Scout was confused so he asked one of the Eagles to explain what was going on.

"Well you see," the Eagle responded, "we've been coming to camp so long that we already know all the jokes. So we listed them with numbers on a piece of paper; now, instead of retelling a joke, we just yell out the number; everyone knows which joke it is, and they laugh."

The new Scout thinks the whole idea is clever and he decides to give it a try. So he stands up and yells, "Fourteen," and the entire room gets quite.

"What did I do wrong," the Scout asked when nobody laughed. "Oh nothing," replied the Eagle, "It's just that some people know how to tell a joke, and some people don't."

***

The highlight of Troop 19 annual winter campout was the ice fishing competition. Each patrol drilled their holes in the ice and began fishing. After several minutes the Black Panther patrol was reeling in one fish after another, while the other patrols continued to have no luck. A young scout approached the Patrol Leader to ask what he was doing wrong.

"Ymm umm wmm umm," the Patrol Leader replied.

"What?" asked the boy again.

"Ymm umm wmm umm," he said again.

"What?"

Finally, the Patrol Leader spit a bunch of worms into his hand and said, "You have to keep the worms warm."

***

The world's smartest man, the Pope, and a Boy Scout were on a transcontinental flight. Suddenly, the pilot burst into the cabin. The plane is going to crash. Grab a parachute and jump. With that he took one of the three parachutes and jumped out of the plane. The world's smartest man said to the Pope and the Boy Scout. "I'm on the verge of developing a cure for cancer. I have a plan for world peace. I'm too important to die." He reached into the closet, slipped his arms into the straps and jumped.

The Pope turned to the Boy Scout and said, "I've lived a long life my son. You take the final parachute."

"Don't worry your holiness," the Boy Scout said. "There are still two parachutes left. When the world's smartest man jumped, he took my knapsack."

***

Two Scouts were walking through the woods when suddenly a mountain lion leaped out in front of them. The first Scout cautioned the second to remain calm. "Remember what we read in the Scout Handbook. If you stand absolutely still, and look the lion straight in the eye, he will turn and run away."

The second Scout said, "Fine, you've read the Scout handbook, and I've read the handbook, but has the lion read the handbook?"

***

A flashlight was charged with assault and battery. At the hearing the judge said, "I'm reducing your charge to simple assault, because in your case, batteries are not included."

Lester Rope stops into town to check out the local watering hole.

"Let me have a root beer please," the rope says to the restaurant owner.

The owner promptly picks up Lester Rope and throws him outside. "We don't serve rope here. Get out and stay out."

The rope moves on to another tavern and has the same experience. Feeling dejected, Lester makes plans to leave town, when another rope approaches him and says, "Hey, what's the matter man, how come you're so down in the dumps?"

Lester Rope replies, "Nobody in this town likes me. I can't even get a restaurant to serve me."

The second rope laughs, "You're going about this all wrong. You need to be hip to get served in a happening town like this." So the second rope instructs Lester to tie himself into a square knot. He then says, "To be really punk, you need to frazzle your hair." So Lester Rope complies, separating his strands to give him the appearance of a punk hair do. With that, he and his new friend go in search of a good time.

"Don't go in there," Lester warns, as they approach one of the restaurants which had earlier refused to serve him. "Don't worry," says the punk rope, "just follow my lead."

So the punk rope steps up to the counter and orders a couple of sodas. The waiter returns and serves them. Eyeing the pair suspiciously, the waiter says, "Hey - wait a minute - are you a rope?"

And the rope replies, "Afrayed knot."

***

A young boy was interested in joining the Boy Scouts, so he went to the meeting hall on the designated night. When he walked in, he found a group of five boys sitting in a circle smoking cigars. Trying not to act surprised the new boy asked, "Is the Scoutmaster around?"

The patrol leader took the cigar out of his mouth, flicked ashes on the floor and asked, "What do you think?"

***

On the first day at camp, the Scoutmaster called together the entire troop. "OK," he asked, "who pushed the outhouse into the river?" No one admitted to doing it. So the Scoutmaster said, "I want to tell you a story about George Washington. When he was a boy he cut down his father's favorite cherry tree. His father asked him if he did it, and when he told the truth, he didn't get into any trouble because he was honest."

"Now we all know good scouts are honest," the Scoutmaster stated. So I'm going ask again, "Who pushed the outhouse into the river?"

The Scoutmaster's son answered, "Father, I cannot tell a lie. I pushed the outhouse in the river."

The Scoutmaster started chasing after his son and screaming at him.

"But dad," the boy cried, "what about George Washington?"

The Scoutmaster responded, "George Washington's father wasn't in the cherry tree."

***

After annoying patrol members with difficult first aid questions, and yelling when questions were answered wrong, a senior patrol leader turned the meeting over to the ASPL. The ASPL reviewed first aid again to prepare the patrol for when the SPL came back for another test. Completing a lengthy discussion on tourniquets, the ASPL asked, "What would you do if the Senior Patrol Leader received a serious head wound?"

"Put a tourniquet around his neck," the patrol replied in unison.

***

During a visit to the local zoo, a Scout from Troop 2 spent nearly an hour trying to awaken a bear. He had hoped to take a picture of the bear in action so that could tell fellow Scouters he had confronted this animal in the wild. When the zookeeper came over the Scout impatiently asked, "What kind of bear is that anyway?"

"Himalayan," the zookeeper replied.

"I know that," screamed the Tenderfoot. "I want to know when him a gettin up."

***

Scouts from Troop 17 were pressed into duty to rescue those folks who may have been trapped in their cabins by an avalanche. After a treacherous journey the rescuers shoveled away enough snow to reach the door of a cabin. Banging loudly, the Scouts said, "We're with the Boy Scouts."

An elderly mountain man responded. "It's been a tough winter boys, and I don't see how I can give you anything this year."

After a week of bad rain, the camp was filled with a variety of insects. All day long mosquitoes bothered the campers, and at night the sky was filled with fireflies.

When one of the younger Scouts saw the fireflies, he turned to his nearby friend and said, "I think we'd better go inside the tent. They're looking for us with flashlights now."

***

Did you hear about the Scoutmaster who threatened to kill his Scouts if they didn't collect the morning mist in a bottle?   It was a case of dew or die.

***

Three Scouts were lost deep in the woods, when they came upon a large white owl sitting in the middle of the trail. To their surprise the owl started speaking, "Weary travelers, he said. I will grant you each one wish.

The first Scout enthusiastically said, "I wish I was home and rich beyond my wildest dreams.

'Your wish is granted," stated the owl.

The second Scout said, "I wish I was home and on a date with the most beautiful girl in the world who was madly in love with me."

"Your wish is granted," said the owl. Then the owl asked the final Scout, "What is your wish?"

"I dunno," said the Scout, "I'm kind of lonely. I wish my friends were still here….."

***

On a dock one day, two Sea Scouts were preparing to get into a boat.

"Can I go downstairs?" one of the younger boys inquired.

"Let's get something straight," the older boy responded. "Downstairs is below deck. Right is starboard. Left is port. The front is the bow and the back is the stern. You need to start using the correct terminology. One more mistake like "downstairs" and I'll throw you out one of those little round windows."

***

The Scoutmaster asked the members of his troop to list three important things they should bring with them on a hike in case they get lost. A neckerchief, pocketknife, food, and matches were all mentioned as important items.   Then Joe Scout suggested a compass, a canteen and a deck of cards.

"I understand the first two items," the Scoutmaster stated, "but what good are a deck of cards when you're lost?"

"Well that's easy," Joe Scout replied.   As soon as you start playing solitaire you can bet someone well come along and say, "Put the red jack on the black queen."

***

A Scoutmaster stopped in to see his Psychiatrist. "Doc you've got to help me. I keep having the same dream over and over again, and I can't get rid of it."

"Tell me about your dream," the psychiatrist inquired.

The Scoutmaster responded, "The first night I dreamt about wigwams. The next night I dreamt about teepees. Then wigwams. Then teepees, then...."

"Wait I minute," the psychiatrist interrupted. "I think I know what your problem is. You're just two tents."

***

A Scoutmaster was very upset so he went to see his Psychiatrist.

"You've got to help me doc," the leader wailed. "I keep having the same dream night after night. There's a door with a sign on it, and I can't push it open."

"What does the sign say?" the Psychiatrist asked.

"Pull."

***

At a camporee a very skinny Senior Patrol Leader met another SPL who was quite overweight.

"From the looks of you," the heavyset Scout stated, "there must have been a famine where you come from."

"From the looks of you," the thin Scout replied, "you must have caused the famine."

Mike and Jim are camping in a remote prairie. After a long day, they set up their tent, go inside and fall fast asleep. Sometime after midnight Mike wakes Jim and says, "Friend, look skyward and tell me, what do you see?"

Jim replies, "I see millions of stars." "And what does that tell you?" asks Mike. Jim grows thoughtful and says, "Astronomically speaking, it tells me there are millions of galaxies and potentially billions of planets. Astrologically, it tells me Saturn is in Leo. Time-wise, it appears to be approximately a quarter past three in the morning. Theologically, it's evident God is all-powerful and we are small and insignificant. Meteorologically, it seems we will have a beautiful day tomorrow.

What's it tell you, Mike?" Mike is silent for a moment, then says, "You idiot. It tells me that someone has stolen our tent! "

***

While visiting a monastery in England the turkey patrol was treated to a traditional British meal, fish and chips. After finishing the meal the Scoutmaster said to the monsignor, "Those were the best fish and chips I've ever had." "Oh don't thank me," said the monsignor, "thank brothers Wesson and Wise." Brother Wesson is the fish friar, and Brother Wise is the chip monk."

***

Troop 7 challenged Troop 21 to a football game. The teams were well matched and the score was tied 0-0 as Troop 7 hiked the ball with just a few minutes left on the clock. Just as the ball was snapped, a train went whirling past the field blowing its horn. The boys from Troop 21 mistook the horn for the signal that time had expired, so they walked off the field.

Three plays later, the boys from Troop 7 scored the winning touchdown.

***

A Scoutmaster was watching a new Scout on his first campout. The Scout reached into his pack and pulled out his dinner; a meal which consisted of a bag of chips, a candy bar, a bottle of soda, and a can of pudding.

"Don't you know the four basic food groups?" the Scoutmaster asked the new Scout.

"Certainly," the boy replied. "Bagged, wrapped, bottled and canned."

A group of Scouters went on a safari in Africa in search of wild game. After several hours they had bagged a variety of animals including a gnu and a rhinoceros. They brought the animals to the tour guide who said he would use them to prepare a wonderful meal.

At dinner the cook served steaks, and the entire party could not get over how good the food was. One of the leaders had heard that Gnu meat was a delicacy in Africa so he asked the Cook, "Is this Gnu?"

"No," answered the Cook, "but it's just as good as Gnu."

***

Did you hear the one about the hermit who got into trouble for driving into town? He was charged with recluse driving.

***

Two Scouts were walking through the woods when suddenly they stumbled upon a large black bear. Immediately, one of the two removed his hiking boots, reached into his pack and slipped on a pair of running shoes. "What are you doing?" his companion asked incredulously. "You know that you can't outrun a bear, even with those on."

"Who cares about the bear," the first hiker replied. "All I need to worry about is outrunning you."

***

There was a Boy Scout named Joe Bajerkolopouliskowski who always hated his name. So he waited and waited for his 18th birthday, and when it arrived, he went down to the courthouse to have his name legally changed.

The clerk asked, "What do you choose as your new name?"

"Lester Bajerkolopouliskowski," he replied.

A Scout fell down a very deep crevasse, breaking both arms. A quick thinking member of his patrol lowered down a rope and instructed the Scout to bite hard onto the rope. Inch by inch, members of the patrol gingerly pulled the Scout toward the top of the crevasse, while he bit firmly on the rope. As he reached the top, the patrol leader called out. "Are you O.K.?"

"Yes,   AAAAAAAAAAAAAAAAAAAHHHHHHHHHH!!!!" he replied.

***

A young Scout was interested in earning the first aid merit badge. As part of the test, the Scoutmaster asked what items should be included in a first aid kit. The Scout listed many items including a jar of mayonnaise.

"Why would you put a jar of mayonnaise in a first aid kit?" the Scoutmaster inquired.

"Because," the young Scout replied, "it says in the Scout Handbook to 'include a dressing.'"

***

Let's get our bearings straight. Directly in front of us is due north. To our right is east, and west is to the left. Now let's see if you guys can figure this out. What's at our backs?

"Knapsacks," the boys of the donkey patrol replied.

Joe Scout

There was a severe blood shortage on the Indian reservation, and the call went out to the local Scouts to donate blood. After arriving at the reservation, Joe Scout was seated on a cot next to an attractive donor who appeared to be a Native American.

"Do you live on the reservation?" Joe Scout asked.

"Yes," replied the young female.

"Are you a full blooded Indian?"

"Well, actually, no," the young women responded. "Right now I'm a pint low."

***

Joe Scout was bragging about the 25-pound trout he had caught while ice fishing. "Twenty-five pounds," the Scoutmaster replied skeptically, "Were there any witnesses?"

"Of course," Joe Scout replied. "Otherwise it would have been a fifty pounder."

***

Joe Scout was telling his fellow Scouts how getting the first aid merit badge had prepared him for an emergency. "I saw a women hit by a truck," he stated. "She had a twisted ankle, broken bones, and a fractured skull."

"How terrible! What did you do?"

"Thanks to my first-aid training, I knew just how to handle it. I sat on the ground, and put my head between my knees to keep from fainting."

***

Joe Scout got careless with matches and lit the field behind his house on fire. Thinking quickly, he ran into the house and called the fire department.

"The field is on fire," Joe Scout cried into the phone.

"Calm down," the dispatcher intoned. "Now how do we get to the field?"

"Don't you still have that red truck?" Joe inquired.

Joe Scout visited Toronto with plans to try his hand at ice fishing. He pitched his tent and got ready to cut a hole in the ice. As he pulled the cord on his chain saw, he heard a voice from above, "There are no fish under the ice."

He pulled the cord again, and the same voice emanated from above, "There are no fish under the ice."

Awestruck, Joe Scout looked reverently at the heavens. "Is that you God," he inquired.

"No," the voice replied. "I own this rink, and I can tell you, there are no fish under the ice."

***

Joe Scout walked down the street carrying a computer and a desk. A police officer walked up to him and said, "I'm afraid I'm going to have to place you under arrest."

"But wait officer," Joe Scout replied, "these items aren't stolen, they belong to me."

"Oh, I realize those items aren't stolen."

"Then what's the charge," Joe Scout queried?

"Impersonating an office, sir."

***

Joe Scout was trying to light a match. He struck one, but it wouldn't light. He struck a second, but it didn't burn either. Finally, he struck a third match and it lit right up. "That's a good one," Joe proclaimed as he blew out the match. "I'll have to save it."

***

Joe Scout was leading his patrol in a hike through the mountains in an effort to complete his orienteering merit badge. After several hours he became hopelessly lost. Unconcerned Joe Scout took out a map and studied it for some time turning it up and down, sighting distant landmarks, checking points on his compass and viewing the position of the sun. After completing what seemed a great effort he finally determined their position. "You see that big mountain over there?" Joe Scout asked as he pointed north. Well according to this map we are standing right on top of it.

***

A women lion tamer had the vicious animals under such complete control that she could command them to take a lump of sugar from her lips and they would obey. Joe Scout stood skeptically by the cage and yelled, "Anyone could do that."

The ringmaster came over and asked, "Would you like to try?"

"Sure," replied Joe Scout. "But first, get those crazy lions out of there!"

***

Two Scouts accompanied Joe Scout for a hike across the desert. The first scout carried a canteen of water; the second scout brought along a loaf of bread. Joe Scout was carrying a car door. A prospector came upon the trio and struck up a conversation. He said to the first Scout, "Why do you have that there canteen of water with you?" "Because there's not much water out here," the first Scout replied.

He turned to the second and asked, "How come you're carrying that there loaf of bread?" The second scout answered, "So I have something to eat when I get hungry."

The prospector then started scratching his head as he turned to address Joe Scout. "Why are you a carryin' that there car door?"

"Well," replied Joe Scout, "so I can roll down the window when it gets hot."

***

Joe Scout ordered a large pizza. The cook pulled the pizza out of the oven and asked Joe Scout, "Do you want me to cut it into 6 or 8 pieces?"

"Better make it six," Joe Scout responded, "I could never eat eight pieces."

***

After breaking his arm, Joe Scout asked the doctor. "Will I be able to play the violin when the cast comes off?" "Of course you will," replied the doctor.

"That's great," stammered Joe. "I always wished I could play the violin."

***

Joe Scout and the members of Troop 00 visited a farm for the first time. "I've been watching that bull over there for some time," Joe Scout related, "and I don't understand how come he doesn't have any horns?"

"Well," replied the farmer, "sometimes we saw off the horns when they're young so the bulls don't poke us. The horns sometimes fall off the older bulls. As for that bull there, the reason why he doesn't have any horns is because he's a horse."

Scout handed his teacher a drawing featuring an airplane covered with grapes, apples, bananas and oranges. Puzzled, the teacher turned to Joe and said, "The theme for today's drawings was supposed to be related to patriotic American songs. How is that drawing related to our topic?"

"You know the song America the Beautiful," Joe Scout replied. "Well that's the fruited plane."

***

Joe Scout ran into the emergency room, jumped on top of the doctor and started yelling, "One, two, three, four."

"What's going on here," the doctor yelled while struggling to free himself.

"Well, doctor," Joe Scout replied. "They told me in admissions that I could count on you."

***

Joe Scout took his little cousin with him when he went fishing. When he got back to the campsite, he was extremely fed up.

"I'm never taking him with me again," Joe complained.

"Did he scare away the fish," the ranger wondered.

"No," muttered Joe Scout. "He sat on the bank all day eating my earthworms."

***

Joe Scout decided to take up painting so he went to the store to buy an easel. At the art supply store they carried two sizes small and large. Joe thought about it for a moment and decided to choose the lesser of two easels.

When Joe Scout first went to camp, a group of boys convinced him to try his hand at elephant hunting. Several hours after he started, he returned to camp empty-handed.

"You didn't catch anything, did ya?" one of the boys asked Joe Scout.

"No, I gave up because the decoys got too heavy," Joe Scout replied.

***

Joe Scout came back to the campsite after a long day of hiking. "My stomach hurts," he complained. "That must be because your stomach is empty," the Scoutmaster reasoned. "You'd feel much better if you had something in it." Later that night the Scoutmaster complained that he was suffering from a terrible headache. "That must be because your head is empty," Joe Scout reasoned. "You'd feel much better if you had something in it."

Once again, the SPL was giving the Albino Polar Bear Patrol a first aid test. Turning to Joe Scout the SPL asked, "What would you do if your sister swallowed the key to your house."

"I'd climb in through the window," Joe Scout replied.

A psychiatrist was questioning Joe Scout. "Do you ever hear voices without being able to tell who is speaking, or where the voices are coming from," he asked.

"All the time," Joe replied.

"And when does this occur?" asked the doctor.

"When I answer the phone."

***

Joe Scout went into the trading post and ordered a gallon of chocolate ice cream. "I'm sorry," replied Trader Jack, "We're all out of Chocolate."

"All right then," Joe replied. "I'll have a pint of chocolate."

"Joe," Trader Jack intoned. "We have strawberry and we have vanilla, but we have no chocolate."

"Well, I'll just have a small chocolate cone then," Joe replied.

"Joe, pay close attention." Trader Jack said. "Can you spell the *van* in vanilla?"

"Sure," Joe replied, "That's easy V-A-N."

"And can you spell the *straw* in strawberry?"

"Certainly," Joe answered. "S-T-R-A-W."

"And how about the *cottonpick* in chocolate?"

"There's no *cottonpick* in chocolate," Joe said.

"Exactly!"

***

"Do you really sell that many jackknifes?" Joe Scout asked Trader Jack, as the boy examined shelf after shelf lined with jackknifes.

"No," Trader Jack responded. "I maybe sell one or two a month. The truth is I'm not a very good knife seller. But the guy who sells me jackknifes; now he's a good Knife seller."

Joe Beagle Scout

The exciting adventures of Joe Scout's dog - Joe Beagle Scout.

Joe Scout took out the gas can and began to refill his lawn mower. As usual, he was not paying much attention to what he was doing. He overfilled the tank, and gasoline formed a pool alongside the mower. Sadly, Joe Beagle, Joe Scout's faithful dog, ran over and lapped up the gasoline. Joe Scout tried to stop the dog, but the beagle ran in a crazed frenzy around the yard. For twenty minutes Joe Scout chased after the dog when suddenly the dog coughed, stopped and passed out on the lawn.

A concerned neighbor rushed over and asked, "What's the matter with your dog?"

"He ran out of gas," Joe Scout replied.

***

"I'm really worried about Joe Beagle," Joe Scout said to the veterinarian. "I dropped some coins on the floor, and before I could pick them up, he ate them." The veterinarian told Joe he would need to leave his dog at the office overnight for observation.

The next morning Joe Scout called to see how his dog was doing. The vet replied, "no change yet."

***

Joe Beagle visited an old western saloon and ordered a drink. The bartender sneered, grabbed his gun and shot Joe Beagle in the foot. "Scram," he snarled, "we don't serve dogs here."

A week later Joe Beagle returned with a bandaged leg and a six shooter. A new man was tending bar. Limping up to the bar, Joe Beagle said, "I'm looking for the man who shot my paw."

***

Joe Beagle walked into the trading post, grabbed a ginger ale, handed the clerk 75 cents, popped open the can, drank it down and walked out. An amazed Scout turned to Jester and asked, "Does that dog always do that?"

"Oh no," Jester replied. "Usually he gets a cola."

Joe Scout and Joe Beagle walked into a restaurant. They were stopped at the door by a waiter who said, "I'm sorry, no dogs allowed." "But wait," responded Joe, "this is a talking dog. I'll ask him three questions, and if he answers them correctly, promise you'll let us stay." The waiter agreed.

Joe asked his dog, "What's the opposite of smooth?"

"R-r-ruff," barked his dog.

"What's on top of a house?"

"R-r-roof", the Beagle responded.

"Right again," cried Joe Scout. "Now who's the best baseball player?"

"R-r-ruth," said the dog.

The waiter then threw Joe Scout and Joe Beagle into the alley saying, "Don't ever come back in here again."

As they lay there, Joe Beagle looked quizzically at Joe Scout and said, "Aaron?"

***

While staying at Scout Camp, Joe Scout and Joe Beagle Scout decided to try some fishing. While grabbing a boat Joe asked the ranger how the fishing was.

"Fishing's great," he replied.

After several hours on the water, Joe Scout hadn't caught a fish. Disgusted he returned the boat to the ranger. "I thought you said the fishing was great," Joe Scout stammered.

"The fishing's always great," replied the ranger, "catchin 'em is what's difficult."

***

Joe Scout and Joe Beagle went hiking and wandered onto some private property. A recluse and his wife encountered the duo and the man began yelling at Joe Scout for trespassing. With that Joe Beagle went over and bit the stranger, then cornered the stranger's wife and did the same.

"I can understand why your dog bit me," the recluse cried. "But why did he have to go off and bite my poor wife."

"To get the bad taste out of his mouth," Joe Scout replied.

A businessman placed a classified ad for a position he had open. The job required a bilingual person who could type, take dictation, and operate a computer.

The first to apply for the position was a dog named Joe Beagle. Not wanting to discriminate, the business owner gave the dog the standard secretarial test. To his surprise, the dog was a wizard with the computer; he took dictation well, and typed nearly 150 words per minute.

"I'm very impressed with your qualifications," the businessman told the dog. "But there is still one requirement. Are you bilingual?"

Joe Beagle barked, wagged his tail, and then answered the question. "Meow," he replied.

***

A woman was eating her lunch by the lake. Joe Scout and his faithful dog Joe Beagle were sitting nearby. Joe Beagle smelled the woman's food and began to whine.

"You don't mind if I throw him a bit, do you?" the women inquired.

"Not at all," Joe Scout replied.

So the women picked Joe Beagle up and threw him in the lake.

***

Joe Scout took his dog Joe Beagle with him to see the movie, *101 Dalmatians*. When the usher noticed the dog he was about to throw him out, but relented when he saw that the animal seemed to be paying very close attention to the film. After the show, the usher went over to Joe Scout. "It certainly surprised me to see your dog enjoying this film, he said.

"It surprised me too," Joe Scout replied. "He didn't like the book at all."

Joe Scout and Jester

Joe and Jester were hiking through the forest. Suddenly the Jester stopped short and took a deep sigh.

"What's wrong," Joe Scout queried?

"Nothing," Jester replied. "But I sure wish Miss Manners was with us."

"Why?" Joe Scout asked.

"Because I think we took the wrong fork."

***

Joe and Jester were standing over a dead man named Juan. "I think he was killed with a golf gun," Jester surmised.

"A golf gun?" wondered Joe Scout. "What's a golf gun?"

"I don't know, but it sure made a hole in Juan."

Jester and Joe Scout grabbed a canoe and decided to go fishing. After a very successful day Jester said, "We really should mark this spot so we can come back tomorrow." So Joe Scout painted an "X" on the bottom of the boat.

"You idiot," Jester jeered. "That's not very smart. What happens if we come back tomorrow and they give us a different boat?"

***

Joe Scout and Jester were tracking a bear along the Appalachian Trail. After some time the tracks disappeared. They decided to continue on in hopes of picking up bear tracks again. After walking a little further along the trail they came to a fork in the path. A sign advised them, bear left. So they decided to go home too.

***

Joe Scout and Jester decided to stop for dinner at an area steak house. Jester ordered a porterhouse steak, Joe Scout asked for a lobster tail. After about 10 minutes the waitress returned with a steak in one hand and a book in the other. She gave the steak to Jester, and then she opened the book and sat down next to Joe Scout.

"Once upon a time", she began, "there was a little lobster."

Joe and Jester bought two horses from a local farm. The horses were very similar, and the two friends could never tell them apart. So they shaved the mane off one horse, but it grew back. They then cut the tail off the other horse, but it also grew back. Exasperated, Joe finally got the clever idea of measuring the height of each horse, because it appeared one horse might be slightly bigger than the other. Sure enough, their problem was solved once and for all. It turns out that the white horse is a quarter of an inch taller than the black one.

***

Jester walked into a fish market and asked the owner to toss him the biggest fish he had. "Why do you want me to throw it to you," the owner asked. Jester responded, "So when I go home I can honestly say that I caught it."

***

Joe Scout and Jester were talking about cooking. "I got me a cookbook once," Joe Scout claimed, "but I never could do a thing with it."

"Too many fancy dishes?" Jester inquired.

"Yup," every one of them started out the same way. "Take a clean dish...and that ended my cooking right there."

***

Joe Scout and Jester stood by the Scoutmaster's car. Foolishly, Joe Scout had locked the leader's keys in the car.

"Why don't we get a coat hanger to open it," Jester inquired.

"Where are we going to find a coat hanger in the middle of the woods?" Joe responded.

"Well what if we just cut the rubber with my pocket knife. Then we could stick our finger down and pull up the lock."

"The Scoutmaster would kill us if we wrecked his window like that."

"Well, we better think of something," Jester replied with a sigh. "It's starting to rain and the sun roof is wide open."

***

Joe Scout and Jester decided to try their hand at tracking animals. After hiking around for a while, they uncovered their first set of tracks. "Them are bear tracks," Joe Scout informed Jester.

"Don't be ridiculous," Jester replied. "Those are obviously deer tracks."

So the two stood there arguing for several hours, until a train nearly hit them.

***

Joe was telling Jester about his trip to the Rockies. Jester asked, "What did you think of the scenery?"

"Oh, I couldn't really see much," Joe explained, "There were too many mountains in the way."

***

At the campfire, Joe Scout announced that he was going to sing one of his favorite tunes, "Over the river and far away."

"Thank goodness," whispered Jester. "I thought he was going to stay here singing all night."

***

During a rainy day at camp Joe Scout began working on a 200-piece jigsaw puzzle. After working on it every night for 2 weeks, the puzzle was finally finished. "Looky what I've done, Jester," Joe Scout shrieked excitedly to his friend.

"That's pretty good, Joe. How long did it take you to do that?"

"Only two weeks," Joe proudly replied.

"Is two weeks fast?" Jester inquired.

"You bet," Joe Scout exclaimed. "Look at the box. It says, from 2 to 4 years."

***

Jester was ironing his Scout uniform while Joe Scout entertained himself watching TV. "I'm going to get a soda" Jester said as he left Joe Scout alone in the living room. When he returned he was surprised to find that Joe Scout had a serious burn on both ears. "What happened?" Jester asked as he glanced at his injured friend.

"Well, I was watching TV when the phone rang. I absentmindedly picked up the iron, and placed it to my ear."

"That's terrible," Jester replied. "How did you burn the other ear?"

"They called back."

Joe Scout and Jester were contemplating sneaking out of camp after dark. When no one was aware, Joe Scout slipped away from the troop to determine if there was a good place to climb over the fence, or to tunnel under it. Joe Scout returned with a disappointed look on his face. "We can't tunnel under, or climb over the fence. I guess we can't leave the camp," he complained.

"Why not," Jester asked.

"Because there's no fence."

At the campfire, Joe Scout volunteered to play his trumpet. The noise was awful. After finishing his first song, Joe asked the group, "Is there anything you would like me to play?"

"Yes," cried Jester. "How about playing dominoes."

***

Joe Scout and Jester were out in their boat one day when a hand appeared in the ocean.

"What's that?" Joe Scout wondered. "It looks as if someone is drowning."

"Nonsense," replied Jester. "It was just a little wave."

***

Joe Scout decided to enroll in truck driving school. At the end of a long day of class the instructor began quizzing Joe Scout on what he had learned. "You're in an eighteen wheeler," the instructor began, "carrying a heavy load barreling down a two lane highway. Jester, your co-driver is asleep. There are eight trucks behind you, and as you come over the top of a hill, they pull out beside you to pass. Suddenly you see several trucks coming in the opposite direction pulling into your lane to pass. What do you do?"

"That's simple," Joe Scout replied. "I'd wake up Jester."

"Why would you do that?" asked the instructor.

"Because," replied Joe Scout, "Jester ain't never seen a truck wreck like this before!"

The Camp Ranger

The camp ranger was walking through a desolate side of camp when he caught wind of something burning in the distance. Farther along the trail he found an elderly hermit cooking a meal.

"What's cooking?" the ranger asked.

"Peregrine Falcon," replied the hermit.

"Peregrine Falcon!" the ranger exclaimed. "Don't you know they are an endangered species, and that it is illegal to eat them?"

"I'm sorry," the hermit said, "but I've had no contact with the outside world in more than 30 years. How could I have known?"

The ranger agreed not to report the old timer this time, but made him promise never to eat falcon again. As he was leaving, curiosity got the best of the old ranger and he asked, "What does Peregrine Falcon taste like anyway?"

"Well", replied the hermit, "it's sort of a cross between bald eagle and whooping crane."

***

After several failed attempts at conventional fishing Joe Scout endeavored to improve his luck. So he went out on the lake and began dropping sticks of dynamite over the side. He waited for the boom and began scooping the fish out with a net.

After he'd done this 3 or 4 times the camp ranger rushed over and said, "Joe, you know you aren't allowed to fish like that."

Joe Scout paid him little attention. Lighting up another stick of dynamite he handed it to the ranger and said, "you gonna talk, or are you gonna fish?"

***

The ranger was out chopping down a dead tree when a short thin man walked by. "That's not the way to chop down a tree," the little guy yelled.

"Oh no," responded the surprised camp ranger. He handed the ax to the other man. "Suppose you show me how it's done." With one swing of the ax, the little guy brought the tree crashing to the ground.

"That's amazing," the ranger stammered. "Where did you ever learn to do that?"

"I used to be a lumberjack in the Sahara forest," the little stranger answered.

"What do you mean the Sahara forest," replied the ranger. "It's the Sahara desert."

"It is now."

The ranger took a group of boys from camp on a white water rafting trip. "Don't be alarmed," he told the Scouts, "I know every rock in the river." Just then, the boat overturned and flipped them all into the river.

"See," said the ranger, "there's one now."

***

The ranger found Joe Scout fishing in the lake right next to a sign that said, "No fishing allowed."

"What's the meaning of this Joe?" the ranger asked?

"Oh I'm not fishing," Joe replied. "I'm just teaching these worms to swim."

***

The Ranger needed to take a short break so he asked Joe Scout to keep an eye on the waterfront. Thirty minutes later he returned to hear Joe Scout making an announcement on the megaphone.

"Boat 99 you've wandered out to far come in please."

The ranger said to Joe, "What are you yelling about. We only have 75 boats. There is no boat number 99."

Without hesitation Joe Scout continued, yelling, "Boat 66 are you in some sort of trouble?"

***

A visitor to camp asked the ranger what time it was. The ranger quickly responded that he thought it was about 12 o'clock.

The surprised visitor wondered, "Only 12 o'clock, I thought it was much later than that."

"Oh, it never gets later than 12 at this camp," the ranger responded.

"How can that be?" the puzzled visitor queried.

"Well, after 12:00," the ranger replied, "it goes back to one again."

***

Joe Scout was walking by a pay phone when it began to ring. He answered it, and went straight to get the ranger. "I think you're wanted on the phone, sir," Joe said to the ranger.

"What do you mean, think?" the ranger asked. "Well," Joe stuttered, "when I answered the phone the voice on the other end said, "Is that you, you old fool?""

The beaver patrol entered the camp after traveling through a remote and rather uninteresting portion of the state. Noticing a "scenic route" sign, the Scouts got into a discussion about whether it would be better to take the longer scenic route, or whether they should continue down the rather uninteresting route they had been traveling. They approached the ranger with the question, "What will we see on the scenic route that we haven't seen so far?"

The ranger asked, "What have you seen so far?"

"Nothing," replied the Scouts.

"Then you've seen most of it already," the ranger responded.

***

"Did anyone lose a roll of money with a rubber band around it," the ranger asked the troops.

Several Scouts eagerly yelled, "I did I did."

"Well I just found the rubber band," the ranger replied.

***

"The sign says no fishing allowed," the ranger said as Joe Scout cast out his line.

"I saw the sign," Joe Scout responded, "so I'm fishing silently."

***

Joe Scout was hiking through the woods with the ranger when they came upon a couple of penguins. "They should be taken to the zoo," the ranger said. Joe Scout agreed, and he and the two penguins left.

The next day the ranger saw Joe Scout and the penguins together. "You were supposed to take them to the zoo," the ranger stated.

"I did," replied Joe Scout. "And tonight I'm taking them to the movies."

***

Joe Scout was again fishing, close to the ranger's watchful eye. He landed a very large trout and gingerly returned it to the lake. Next he caught a pickerel, but he threw that back too. After that he reeled in a little tiny bass, and with a smile, he placed the little bass on his stringer.

The ranger was confused. "Why did you keep that tiny fish after returning the others?"

Joe Scout answered, "Because I only brought my small frying pan to camp."

The Ranger was walking through camp when he spotted Chief Sequassen banging a stick against a hollow log.

"What are you doing," the ranger inquired?

"Calling log distance", the Chief answered.

The Cubs Have It

A Cub Scout returned from a horse ranch and described to his parents all he had seen. "I even saw a man who builds horses," the Cub excitedly explained.

"Are you sure?" the boy's parents inquired.

"Yes, when I got there I saw he had one almost finished, he was just nailing on the feet."

***

Two Boy Scouts were trying to measure a pole. They tried various ways to scale the pole but neither could get to the top with a tape measure. After an hour they were about to give up when a Cub Scout wandered by.

"What are ya doing?" the Cub asked.

"Trying to determine the exact height of this pole," one of the Scouts answered.

"Why don't you just lay it on the ground and measure it that way?" the Cub asked.

The Boy Scouts just shook their heads. "That's a really dumb idea. We want to know how high the pole is, not how long," the Scouts answered.

***

When the Camp was first being explored, a group led by Robert Judd rode into camp on horseback. Being unfamiliar with the area, they became lost before too long. Suddenly Chief Sequassen came up to them on horseback. Immediately behind him was a small black bear also riding a horse. Confused, Robert Judd asked them which way to go. Unsure himself, Chief Sequassen sent the bear ahead to check the area out. Before long the small bear returned and drew a detailed map of the area. Robert Judd was impressed saying, "I didn't think that little bear could do that."

Chief Sequassen replied, "Haven't you ever seen a Cub Scout?"

A young Cub Scout walks up to the Cubmaster after a pack meeting and says, "When I grow up, I want to be a Cubmaster just like you. So could you please do a better job?"

A group of Eagle Scouts scaled Mount Washington and returned to tell of their arduous trip.

One of the Eagles explained to a group of parents how very high the mountain was.

Another Eagle Scout talked about the steepness of the trail, and the danger the boys faced fighting thin air and fatigue.

"Oh I know how difficult Mount Washington can be," one of the parents responded. "I took my Tiger Cub troop there last year...."

***

A Cub Scout ran to the store for his mother and took his time coming home. A neighbor spotted him and said, "Aren't you late for supper, your mother's been looking for you."

"Don't worry," replied the Cub. "I'm not late for supper, I've got the food."

Chief Sequassen

A turtle went to see Chief Sequassen. "I'm terribly shy," the turtle confessed to the wise old chief. "Can you cure me?"

"Absolutely," said Chief Sequassen. "I'll have you out of your shell in no time."

***

Many moons ago Chief Sequassen traveled to visit a tribe on the eastern shore of Lake Michigan. Shortly after he arrived, a huge pillar of smoke came billowing across the lake.

"Oh wise Chief Sequassen," a young brave asked, "can you explain the meaning of this smoke signal?"

The Old Chief studied it for a moment and then replied, "I've not often seen signals in this dialect, but apparently it says a Mrs. O'Leary has had some trouble with her cow."

***

A group of Indian chiefs had gathered and were sitting around the campfire telling stories. "We have a young brave in our tribe," one chief said who never forgets anything. "The devil can have my soul if I'm not telling the truth."

Later that night the devil visited the Indian Chief. "Come along with me and let's find out if I'm going to get your soul." They went together to visit the young brave. "Do you like eggs?" the devil inquired of the brave.

"Yes," the young Indian responded.

The devil was poised to ask another question when a legion of goblins called him away on other business. Twenty-five years later, the old chief died, and the devil dashed off in search of the brave.

"How," said the devil, his right arm raised in Indian fashion.

"Over-easy," replied the brave.

***

Once there was an Indian whose name was Shortcake. He lived with his wife, Squaw. Sadly, Shortcake died. Chief Sequassen wandered over to Squaw to see what she would do with the dead body. She replied, "Squaw bury Shortcake."

A builder decided to clear a wooded area in order to build a new golf course. Shortly after the project started Chief Sequassen, who lived nearby, wandered up to the foreman and said, "Rain tomorrow."

Sure enough, the next day it rained.

A week later Chief Sequassen again visited the workman and said, "Storm tomorrow." The following day there was an incredible hailstorm.

The foreman said to his assistant. That Indian is incredible. When we lay down the greens we will need 3 consecutive days of nice weather. You'd better hire that Indian to tell us when we can lay the greens.

Chief Sequassen successfully predicted several more storms, but then unexpectedly, stopped coming by. The foreman was anxious to lay the final greens so he sent for Chief Sequassen.

When the Chief finally came, the foreman began. "I rely on your wisdom," the foreman stated. "What will the weather be like tomorrow?"

Chief Sequassen shrugged and said, "I don't know, my radio is broken."

***

A pilot was flying over Chief Sequassen's reservation when he began having trouble with his engine. Thinking fast he put on his parachute and bailed out of the plane, floating gently to the ground. Unfortunately, he landed right in the Old Chief's cooking pot, which was simmering gently over a fire. The surprised chief looked at the pilot and asked, "What's this flier doing in my soup?"

***

Chief Sequassen was sending smoke signals, when suddenly he put aside his regular blanket and began using a baby blanket.

"What's that for?" a bystander asked.

"I'm making small talk," Chief Sequassen responded.

***

Chief Sequassen was riding his horse on the open prairie when he stumbled upon an Indian with his ear to the ground. Chief Sequassen got down from his horse and put his ear to the ground. After a few minutes he spoke. "I don't hear anything," the Chief stated.

"I know," the Indian replied, "It's been like this all day."

It Isn't Easy Being a Scoutmaster

The Scoutmaster always believed that five was his lucky number. He was born on May 5ᵗ 1955. He had 5 children. He lived at 555 West 55ᵗʰ street. On his 55ᵗʰ birthday he went to the track, and he was surprised to find a horse named Numero Cinco running in the fifth race. So 5 minutes before the race, he went to the fifth window and put down $5,555 on Numero Cinco.

Sure enough, the horse finished fifth.

***

On the first day of the national Jamboree, Scoutmasters from all over the country gathered for a cracker barrel. A Scoutmaster from Massachusetts spent the whole evening listening to a Scout leader from Texas brag about the heroes of the Alamo. Finally, the Texan said, "I'll bet you never had anyone that brave in Boston."

"Haven't you ever heard of Paul Revere?" asked the Bostonian.

"Paul Revere?" said the Texan. "Oh, yeah; wasn't he the guy who ran for help?"

***

A Scoutmaster was racing along Interstate 95 at ninety-five miles an hour when he was pulled over by a state trooper. "Why were you going so fast," the trooper inquired?

"Well," the Scoutmaster replied, "I saw the sign back there that said 95 and I was just doing the speed limit."

"Well," the trooper sighed. "It's a good thing I caught you before you got to Interstate 395."

***

A Scoutmaster saw a group of young Scouts gathered around a small cat. "What are you boys up to," the Scoutmaster inquired.

"Trading lies," one of the Scouts replied. "We found this cat and whoever can tell the biggest lie will get to keep the kitten."

"Why when I was your age, I would never think of telling lies," the Scoutmaster said incredulously.

"Okay, you win," the scouts unanimously cried. "The cats yours."

The Scoutmaster asked each patrol to put together a list of who, in their opinion, were the 9 greatest Americans of Today. After about 20 minutes the Scoutmaster visited the Panther Patrol. "Have you finished your list yet?" he wondered.

"No, not yet. We still can't decide on a center fielder."

***

The Scoutmaster noticed that Joe Scout had been daydreaming through the entire first aid training session. He decided to try and get Joe's full attention. "Joe," he said, "If a fire truck is red, and first aid kits are 2 for ten dollars, how old am I?"

"Thirty-four," Joe answered with hesitation.

"That's amazing," the Scoutmaster responded. "How did you ever guess?"

"That's easy," Joe replied. "My older brother is seventeen and he's only half crazy."

***

A Scoutmaster walked into a train station and requested a ticket to the moon. "I'm sorry," the agent reported, "but the moon is full."

***

"That's wonderful keeping a lion and a monkey in the same cage," said the Scoutmaster who was visiting a small zoo. "How do they get along?"

"Okay usually," answered the zookeeper. "Occasionally they have a disagreement and we need to get a new monkey."

The Trading Post

It was a sweltering day, and Hermit the Frog was as hot as he could be. So he went to the trading post to see if his friend, Patty Wack, would let him have an ice cream cone. "Can I have some ice cream," Hermit asked as he walked to the window. "You know the rules," Patty responded, "what have you got to trade." Hermit searched his bag for something with which to barter. All he could find was a dusty Indian statue. "How about this?" Hermit croaked.

"I'll have to ask Trader Jack," Patty replied.

Patty explained the situation and handed Trader Jack the statue. Then she asked if she should accept the statue in exchange for some ice cream.

Trader Jack responded, "That's a knick-knack, Patty Wack, give the frog a cone."

***

A group of Scouts visited the trading post, and found an Indian delivering necklaces for sale. "Excuse me," one of the Scouts asked, "but what's this necklace made of?"

"Alligator teeth," the Indian replied.

"I guess they must be valuable to you like pearls are to us," the boy stated.

"Not quite," replied the Indian. "Just about anybody can open an oyster."

***

A Scout sat in the trading post playing checkers with Big Foot. A stranger came in and stood watching them play in complete amazement. When they finished their game he came over and said, "I'm a television reporter. You and your big hairy friend here could make a fortune in Washington, D.C." The Scout just shrugged. "He's not that clever," the Scout said dismissively. "I've just beaten him two out of the last three games."

***

A man walked into the snack bar at the trading post. "Bring me a turtle sandwich," he demanded, "and make it snappy."

Two old college friends ran into each other at the trading post after many years apart. The first man asked the second, "What have you been up to all these years."

The second man replied, "My life has been crazy. Believe it or not, I've been married four times. I married a millionaire first, then an actress, followed by a seamstress and then a mortician."

"That's a strange combination," said the first man. "Why did you marry them?"

"Well," the second man replied, "it was one for the money, two for the show, three to get ready and four to go."

***

Two Trout were dining at the trading post when one of them started to wave his empty glass in the air. The waiter turned to the busboy and said, "I think there's two fish out of water at table 5."

***

A customer went to the trading post and ordered a well-done steak. But when the waiter served it, the steak was very rare. Angry, the customer called out, "Didn't you hear me say, "well done?""

"No, but thank you," replied the waiter. "I don't get many compliments."

***

A boy was brought to court for stealing a backpack from the trading post. He told the judge that it wasn't his intention to keep the backpack, he had just taken it as a joke to see if it would be missed.

"Since you took it all the way home," the judge answered, "I'm going to give you 30 days for carrying a joke too far."

Two eggs, an English muffin and 3 sausages walk into the trading post. "Let me have a soda for each of my friends," says one of the eggs.

I'm sorry," Traded Jack replied. "We don't serve breakfast."

The Wild Adirondack Cow

For those who do not live in the Northeast, this section requires a special introduction. The Wild Adirondack Cow is a carnivorous moose-like creature that inhabited the Adirondack and Berkshire valleys. Similar to a Holstein in shape and color, the much larger Wild Adirondack Cow features a wide jaw and bear-like teeth. Most scientists believe the Wild Adirondack Cow (WAC) is now extinct, nonetheless, many campers claim to have seen the creature in recent times. Tales about this vicious relative of the grizzly bear are a central theme in Indian folklore.

Troop 45 was out hiking in the woods. Suddenly they spotted what appeared to be a living Wild Adirondack Cow. With great excitement the Scoutleader grabbed his cellular phone and tried to contact the nearest zoo. After waiting and waiting he dialed the operator and demanded, "Why can't I get through to the zoo?"
"Sorry sir," replied the operator. "Lion's busy."

***

After much effort the Indians developed a method of making wool out of Wild Adirondack Cow's milk. Unfortunately, it made the cows feel a little sheepish.

***

A Wild Adirondack Cow went to see the eye doctor because he kept bumping into things.
"You need glasses," said the doctor.
"Will I be able to read with them?"
"Yes," the doctor replied.
"That's great," replied the Wild Adirondack Cow. "I always wished I could read."

"I thought I told you to draw a picture of a Wild Adirondack Cow eating grass," said the art merit badge counselor. "Why have you handed in a blank sheet of paper?"

"Because the cow ate all the grass, that's why there's no grass."

"But what about the Wild Adirondack Cow?"

"There wasn't much point in him hanging around when there was nothing to eat so he went into the forest."

"Why are you tearing up your handbook and scattering it around the camp?" the furious leader asked.

"To keep Wild Adirondack Cows away."

"There are no Wild Adirondack Cows at this camp," snapped the Scoutmaster.

"Shows how effective it is, doesn't it?"

***

Did you hear about the Wild Adirondack Cow that ate bits of metal every night?   It was his staple diet.

***

Three animals were sitting in the forest debating over which was the most feared. The first, a hawk, claimed animals feared him because he could repeatedly attack undetected from above. The second animal, a lion, said he was king of the feared animals because he possessed superior speed and strength. The skunk insisted he was feared above the others because he could frighten away animals without needing flight, nor strength. As the group argued, A Wild Adirondack Cow appeared, and proved he was the most feared animal that ever lived. Before they could utter another word, he ate them all - hawk, lion and stinker.

***

Did you hear that revolutionary war soldiers sent a group of Wild Adirondack Cows into space to orbit the earth? Apparently, it was the herd shot round the world.

Trader Jack's Jokes

When it came time to migrate north, two elderly vultures doubted they had the energy to make the trip so they decided to go by plane. When they checked their baggage, the attendant noticed they were carrying two dead armadillos. "Do you want to check the armadillos as luggage?" he asked.

"No thanks," the vultures replied. "They're carrion".

***

Two farmers were discussing their cattle. One inquired, "What did you give your bull last year when it was sick?"

"Fed him kerosene," the farmer responded. They then went on their separate ways.

Months later, the farmers met again. The first farmer said, "Say Jake, you told me you fed your bull kerosene when he was sick. I gave that to mine and he died."

"Yep," Jake responded, "killed mine too."

***

Did you hear about the ship bound for New York filled with yo-yos that got caught in a violent storm? It sank 25 times.

***

A bus carrying all the local congressmen was speeding down a country road. After passing a small farmhouse, the bus swerved into a field and hit a huge oak tree. A farmer ran out of the farmhouse to investigate the crash. Then he dug a hole and buried all the politicians. A few days later, the local sheriff drove by in search of the missing congressmen, and he saw the damaged bus. He got the farmer, and asked him what happened to all the politicians. The farmer said, "I buried them." The surprised sheriff wondered, "Were they all dead?" The farmer replied, "Some of them were trying to tell me they weren't, but you know how politicians lie!"

***

Did you hear about the cross-eyed teacher that had no control over his pupils?

A newly hired musician was having trouble keeping the beat with the ship's orchestra. The captain grew annoyed and finally threatened the new musician. "Either you learn to keep time or I'll throw you overboard. It's up to you; sync or swim."

***

Once there was a boy whose parents named him Odd. Throughout his life, everyone teased him about his name. As he grew old, he wrote out his final wishes. "I've been the butt of jokes all my life," he said. "I don't want people making fun of me after I'm gone." He asked to be buried in the middle of the wilderness with a tombstone that does not bear his name.

After his death, people stumbled upon the large blank stone and said, "That's odd."

***

An American Boy Scout visited Great Britain. He entered the lobby of a hotel and pushed the button to call the elevator. After a lengthy wait, he grew impatient and asked, "Why is there such a delay?"

The hotel clerk responded, "Be patient, the lift will be down directly."

"The lift?" replied the American Scout. "Oh, you mean the elevator."

"No, I mean the lift," replied the Englishman, annoyed by the American's arrogant attitude.

"I think I should know what it is called," said the American. "After all, elevators were invented in the United States."

"Perhaps," retorted the Englishman. "But the language was invented here."

***

Two goats were snooping around the back of a video rental store when they came upon a discarded videotape. One goat hungrily devoured the tape. His companion watched him and, when he had finished asked, "How was it?"

The first goat replied, "Frankly, the book was better."

An Atheist was walking through a very desolate part of the northern forest. Suddenly, he heard a ferocious howl as Big Foot sprung onto the path directly to his rear. The creature picked him up and hurled him to the ground. The Atheist got up and began to run with all his might in an attempt to escape the attacking creature. As the Big Foot once again drew near, the atheist cried out, "Oh God, help me, save me."

At once the skies opened and the brutal attack scene froze in place with Big Foot's hairy arms and dangerous claws just inches away from the Atheist. A booming voice came from the sky, "I thought you didn't believe in me."

"Oh please, God, give me a break," the man pleaded. "Up until 10 minutes ago, I didn't believe in Big Foot either."

***

Long ago Chief Sequassen was about to die so he called for Rugged Mountain and Falling Rocks, the two bravest warriors of the tribe. The Old Chief instructed each to go out and seek buffalo skins. Whoever returned with the most skins would be the chief. About a month later Rugged Mountain returned with one hundred pelts, but Falling Rocks never returned. Even today has you drive down the highways that pass through the old tribal territory you can see signs that say: Watch out for Falling Rocks.

***

A Kansas farmer died and left his entire estate to his only son. Twenty-four hours later, the bank foreclosed on the farm.

"Well," stammered the son, "Dad did say that the farm would be mine one day."

***

Three elderly sisters had lived together all their lives and they were getting very forgetful. One went upstairs to take a bath. She filled the tub, stepped in with one foot and said, "Was I getting into the tub or getting out? I'll have to ask my sister." She called for her sister and asked, "Was I getting into the tub or getting out?" The sister replied, "I don't know, I'll come upstairs and look!" As she started to go upstairs, she said, "Was I going up the stairs or coming down? I'll have to ask my sister. Was I going up the stairs or down the stairs," she inquired of sister number three. "I don't know," she replied. "Thank goodness I'm not forgetful like my other two sisters, she said as she knocked on wood. "Was that the front door or the back door?"

A young brave walked up to Chief Sequassen while he was sending smoke signals. The brave wondered aloud. How come you have two campfires, a large and a small one?

I use the small one for local calls, and the big one for long distance.

***

"Tell me," the priest asked a cannibal. "Do you think religion has made any progress here?"

"Absolutely," the native replied. "Now we only eat fisherman on Fridays."

***

A doctor tells his patient, "I've got some good news and some bad news for you." So the patient asks, "What's the good news Doc?"

And the doctor says, "They're going to name a disease after you."

***

A waiter in a large restaurant was stricken and rushed to a nearby hospital's emergency room. On the operating table and in great pain, he waited for attention. An intern who had recently been to the restaurant passed by. The patient pleaded, "Help me, Doc. Can't you do something?"

"I'm sorry," the intern retorted. "This isn't my table."

Order your Scout Fun Books today!

Scout Riddles

Superior Campfires

The Scout Puzzle & Activity Book

Scout Skits

Scout Jokes

Scoutmaster's Minutes

Scoutmaster's Minutes II

More Scout Skits

Along the Scouting Trail

Campfire Tales

Run-ons and Even More Scout Skits

Scout Games

For an updated list of available books along with current pricing visit: *scoutfunbooks.webs.com*
or find our books on Amazon!

Books are also available on a wholesale basis to qualified Scout Troops, Council Shops, trading posts in quantities of 50 or more. Contact us by email at BoyScoutBooks@aol.com.

Made in America

8831896R00026

Printed in Great Britain
by Amazon.co.uk, Ltd.,
Marston Gate.